RU
FRAGMENTS ECSTASIES

RUMI
FRAGMENTS ➔ ECSTASIES

Translations by
Daniel Liebert

OMEGA PUBLICATIONS
NEW LEBANON

Second Edition / First Printing
isbn 0-930872-64-7

Published by Omega Publications
256 Darrow Road
New Lebanon NY 12125-2615

Front cover typography by Barkat Curtin
Line drawing by Tom Stier
Book design by Abi'l-Khayr

We invite you to explore other materials
by and about Jelaluddin Rumi
and the Sufi tradition
at our website:
www.wisdomschild.com

PREFACE

1244... the town of Konya, in what is now Turkey...
Rumi, a sober Islamic pedagogue, first gazes into the
face of a ragged dervish, Shams al-Din, "The Sun Of
Tabriz." In that face Rumi sees the image of the
timeless Beloved and till the end of his life he turns,
bewildered with love, shattered, magnificent, angelic.
His humility awesome, deiform. His message simple:
"your helplessness and need are the Way."

After 1247, when Shams al-Din vanished, Rumi
created the turning dance of the Mevlevi dervishes to
exemplify the search for the lost Beloved. In the
ecstatic trance of the 'Sema', this dance to wailing
flute and pacing drum, Rumi extemporaneously
recited thousands of odes which students hastily
transcribed. Most of the material translated here is
from the *Divan*, a book of these ecstatic odes. Other
fragments are from the *Mathnavi*, Rumi's epic and
definitive poem on the Sufi Way.

➡

RUMI
FRAGMENTS → ECSTASIES

ONE

---

the flute weeps
to the pacing drum

the drunken camel
rises from its knees
and tugs at the rope of reason

the bird flutters
in the heart's cage
putting out his head
on this side and that

the flood fills
the ancient riverbed
and once again
the riverbanks are green

the falcon hears
the royal drum
and circles seeking
the wrist of the king

the musk deer
smells the lion

and her haunches are trembling

the madmen have seen
the moon in the window;
they are running to the roof
with ladders

somewhere tonight
a dervish cries
            "it was my soul
            in the wine!
            it was my soul!"

TWO

---

that moon has come
that moon face of Joseph

if you haven't any eyes
go borrow them from someone

when you see that face
you'll no longer care for sightseeing

you more resemble Joseph
than all that is high or low

by God, when you see your beauty
you'll be the idol of yourself

don't run off chattering
from the silence

don't go haggling
there is no other market

here, one rose buys a garden
one penny buys a goldmine

for the sea is in love with the drop
the sun is in love with the candle

the Joseph of the heart
is in the pit of the body

and the bedouin buys him
for eighteen coins

THREE

---

we came whirling
out of nothingness
scattering stars
like dust

the stars made a circle
and in the middle
we dance

the wheel of heaven
circles God
like a mill

if you grab a spoke
it will tear your hand off

turning and turning
it sunders
all attachment

were that wheel not in love
it would cry
      "enough! how long this turning?"

every atom
turns bewildered

beggars circle tables
dogs circle carrion
the lover circles
           his own heart

ashamed,
I circle shame

a ruined water wheel
whichever way I turn
is the river

if that rusty old sky
creaks to a stop
still, still I turn

and it is only God
circling Himself

FOUR

I am the student;
teach my contorted face
to smile

make my stupidity
your burden

sew this rag
on that robe

sometimes
you confiscate everything
like a tax-collector
sometimes
you walk ahead
like a guide

sin
and remorse
and sin again;
a fish out of water
flops this way and that

FIVE

---

a woman is God shining
through subtle veils

haughty spirit astride
the elegant mare
of her body

loving her
you love spirit
        not a corpse

spirit is for lovers
        the corpse is for necrophiles

heart's ease, laughter
meaningfulness, love...

Friend! you desire formless things
you are seeking the beloved
        and don't even know.

SIX

---

within me is an ocean
where a thousand Rumis drown
with all their sorrow

worlds within worlds;
dreamers concoct entire Baghdads
from their breasts

asleep or waking
where have you seen yourself
mirrored completely?

a dreamer wanders
from room to room
only to awaken
            in another sort of room

another sort of dawn
comes white as camphor
to show you complete

and a cold wind

            breast-burnishing wind

SEVEN

---

come out from the circle of time
and into the circle of love

enter the street of taverns
and sit among the drunkards

if you want a secret eye
just shut your eyes

if you desire an embrace
just open your arms

if you crave a living face
smash the stone face

why pay the dowry of life
for this old hag, earth?

a thousand generations
have enjoyed what you enjoy

taste a sweetness in your mouth
that was before honey or bee

---

look! here's a bargain;
give one life, and take a hundred!

EIGHT

---

love says,
"I will deliver you this instant!"

I groped for excuses
but love came
excusing me

I don't feel strange anymore
with my heart here
my soul there

I discovered
He is heart and soul

It was He, not I,
knocking at the door
it was He within

I caress my own breast
for there He is hidden

no one else knows you;
since you are I,
I know you

forms become a trifle
when feeling and intuition
richly intensify

in the end
a man tires of everything
except heart's desiring,
soul's journeying

sultan, saint, pickpocket;
love has everyone by the ear
dragging us to God
by secret ways

I never knew
that God, too, desires us

NINE

---

where is there a Rumi
to do good or evil?

if the Beloved comes
I am Muslim

if the Beloved goes
I am infidel

out of all this world
I chose you

I can only be
what you make me

I am a pen
in your hands

what I see
is only what you show

what I have
is only what you give

Beloved, what do you seek
in my pocket and sleeve?

TEN

come, beggars
sit with open hands
at the gate
of nothingness

God will bring bread
without the medium
of bread

sweetness
without honey or bee

when past and future
dissolve
there is only you

senseless as a lute
upon the breast of God

ELEVEN

---

what is this fragrance?
is it from heaven?
whose laughter is this?
is it Houris in paradise?

what wedding is this
with moon for a platter
and heaven for a veil?

what banquet is this
that the Sultan of Baghdad
licks the platters
in our kitchen?

God alone knows!

but come! take a pick-axe
and break apart
your stony self

the heart's matrix
is glutted with rubies

springs of laughter
are buried in your breast

unstop the wine-jar,
batter down the door
to the treasury
of non-existence

the water in your jug
is brakish and low

smash the jug
and come to the river!

TWELVE

Shams al-Din
I went from town to town
and did not see
one such as you

I was a corpse
and now I am new

Joseph, I come
as a mirror
nothing more,

can you really say
I have heard your voice?

can you really say
I have seen your face?

THIRTEEN

---

the weeping flute
remembers
the riverbed

the stick beats the drum,
    "I was once green,
      a living branch."

the skin on the lute
trembles
like living flesh

the lovers turn
bewildered
like Jacob seeking Joseph

if you heard their cries
your heart would shatter
like glass

FOURTEEN

---

as your sword
comes down on my neck
my eyes
will not turn
from your face

when my mouth
is bandaged shut
and this body
laid in the dirt
my eyes
will not turn
from your face

I ask nothing
nothing of you
but your beauty
        your imperious beauty

FIFTEEN

a woman, entirely spirit,
is perfecting our desire
into agony

Joseph shines
in the body's pit

the halvah boy weeps
and the sea of compassion
surges

even the vile worship
in the intricacies
of hell

willingly, unwillingly
we all melt
into God

the lovers melt together
like the mingled light
of a hundred lamps

and you?

our caravan moves on
and you are the campfire
burning out on the sand

alone

between heaven and earth

SIXTEEN

---

in death I lose a body
and He will lose
my phantasies of Him

I go shirtless
to this lovemaking

my body becomes all soul
every hairtip alive

love, enter this body's house
or I must leave it
to seek you

my soul is a ship
scudding the waves
in pursuit of love

be drunk on love
for love is all that exists

mother and father played at love
and one such as you

sprang from nothingness

day and night are in love
each has caught the other's foot
and they go around

at the sound of love's flute
even the dead
tear apart their shrouds
with desire

SEVENTEEN

rock, plant, animal;
to each I have died
and become more,
when have I become less
by dying?

Now I am man.

when I die I will soar with angels
and when I die to the angels
what I shall become
        you cannot imagine.

from dead stinking semen
love formed you

it was love that dragged you howling
from the blood-drinker's womb
to the nursemaid's breast
and from breastmilk
to roast meat and wine
        and the nursemaid's beauty

it is love that drags
this embryo soul
out of the body
   and into paradise

EIGHTEEN

---

the fragrant air
steals the water
from the cistern

each breath pilfers
a fragment of soul
to another world

suddenly
this body is still
like sea-scum
come to rest on the shore

death is shouting
and beating his drum

death is hoarse from shouting

the drum of death
is split
by amazing blows

as you slip beneath the waves
like a shipload of dung

NINETEEN

---

you suspect this could be yours
with a little contrivance

only death to contrivance
will avail you

something good or bad
always comes out of you
it is agony to be still;
the spool turns
when mind pulls the thread

let the water settle;
you will see moon and stars
mirrored in your being

when the kettle boils
fire is revealed
when the millstone turns
the river shows its power

put the lid on the kettle
and be filled
with the boiling of love

TWENTY

---

you embrace some form
saying, "I am this."

By God, you are not this
or that or the other

you are "Unique One"
        "Heart-ravishing"

you are throne and palace and king
you are bird and snare and fowler

like water in jar and river
are in essence the same

you and spirit are the same

your every idol
prostrates
before you

your every thought-form
perishes
in your formlessness

TWENTY-ONE

Why cling to one life
till it is soiled and ragged?

The sun dies,
squandering a hundred lives
every instant

God has decreed life for you
and He will give
        another and another and another.

TWENTY-TWO

---

subtle degrees
of domination and servitude
are what you know as love

but love is different
it arrives complete
just there
like the moon in the window

like the sun
of neither east nor west
nor of anyplace

when that sun arrives
east and west arrive

desire only that
        of which you have no hope
seek only that
        of which you have no clue

love is the sea of not-being
and there intellect drowns

this is not the Oxus River
or some little creek
this is the shoreless sea;
here swimming ends
always in drowning

a journey to the sea
is horses and fodder and contrivance
but at land's end
the footsteps vanish

you lift up your robe
so as not to wet the hem;
come! drown in this sea
a thousand times

the moon passes over
the ocean of non-being

droplets of spray tear loose
and fall back on the cresting waves

a million galaxies

---

are a little scum
on that shoreless sea

TWENTY-THREE

the moon offers light without a hand

the sun is proof of the sun

writing about love
my pen splinters

expounding love
the ass of intellect
lays down in the mire

when He comes
not one hair of me remains

the shadow loves the sun
but when the sun comes
it vanishes

there is no dervish
in all the world
and if there is a dervish
       he doesn't exist

TWENTY-FOUR

---

joy, sorrow,
what's the difference now?

where are your tears
to show him when he comes?

if you haven't any tears
cut your hands to pieces
like the women with Joseph

if you have neither tears
nor desire
then just look:

see these worlds
spinning out of nothing

this is within your power!

RUMI
→ LECTURES →

Whatever men chatter about these days, it is not
love's way.

God gave the blind man a stick so that he may grope
to a Jesus and gain sight.

Look at all the blind men bashing one another with
the stick of intellect!

Some even swing the stick at He who gave the stick!

How proud they are when they blacken a little page
with writing.

Their minds are so shabby that they must graft on a
hundred other minds to make them work, and
this they call 'great learning.'

They elucidate every sort of substance, but of their
own substance they are more ignorant than
donkeys.

All of their sciences together are a little bunch of

posies from our garden.

All of their thoughts are but husks and leaves on a
river of mind that flows from a secret garden.

If the Houri of paradise should nibble his ear,
he cries, "Hey, what's hurting my ear?"

If the sweet basil touches his face, he brushes it
away saying, "Hey, what's bothering
me now?"

He rides his horse from door to door, asking,
"Has anyone seen my horse?"

➜

Sheba sent a gift of forty loads of gold to Solomon. When she reached the land of Solomon, she saw that the mountains and fields, even the dust in the road were pure gold. Day after day she rode on gold until gold lost all value for her. When Solomon saw her gift, he laughed,

"When did I ever ask for porridge from you? I did not ask for gifts; I asked that you be worthy of those gifts I will give you."

➥ THE KEY ➥
RUMI'S ESSENTIAL TEACHING

What is bounty without a beggar?
Generosity without a guest?
Be beggar and guest; for beauty is seeking a
mirror, water is crying for a thirsty man.

→

Hopelessness and need are a tasteful bezel
for that ruby. Your poverty is a Burak;
don't be a coffin riding on other men's shoulders.

→

Thank God! you hadn't the means
or you may have been a Pharaoh.
The prayer of Moses was,
"Lord, I am in need of Thee!"

→

The Way of Moses is all
hopelessness and need
and it is the only way to God.

From when you were an infant,
has hopelessness ever failed you?

Joseph's path leads into the pit;
don't flee across the chessboard of this world,
for it is His game and we are
checkmate! checkmate!

Hunger makes stale bread
more delicious than halvah.
Your discomfort is spiritual indigestion;
seek hunger and passion and need!

A mouse is a nibbler.
God gave him mind in proportion to his needs.
Without need God gives nothing.

How will you impress God?
You are a hundred thousand dinars
in His debt!

➜

A beggar shows his blindness and palsy,
he does not say, "Give me bread, oh People!
I am a rich man with granaries and palaces!"

➜

Bring a hundred sacks of gold
and God will say,
"Bring the heart."

➜

And if you bring a dead heart
carried like a coffin on your shoulders,
God will say,
"Oh, cheat! is this a graveyard?
Bring the live heart! Bring the live heart!"

If you haven't any knowledge
and only opinions,
have good opinions about God.
This is the way.

If you can only crawl,
crawl to Him.

If you cannot pray sincerely,
offer your dry, hypocritical,
agnostic prayer;
for God in His mercy accepts bad coin.

If you have a hundred doubts of God,
make them into ninety doubts.
This is the way.

Oh, Seeker! though you have
broken your vows a hundred times,
come again! come again!
For God has said,
"Though you are on high or in the pit
consider me, for I am the Way."

No Longer Drunk, But the Wine Itself

the gnat
is in the wine jar
he is no longer drunk
he is wine itself

the ambergris
sits in the fire
turning to fragrance

the grain falls
under the millstone
and is lost
in the measure

the cat
is in the gunnysack
swinging high and low

the sugar sack is ripped
spilling sugar
everywhere

I am so ruined
with love

that beggar children
stone me in the alleys

I am so mad with love
that madmen say,
"Be still!"

This village is so poor
even the taxman
doesn't come here

I am gone from your world
where swords clash
over bread

I steal pearls
from a Sultan
not cloth
from the tailor

I am melting
in meaningfulness
like sugar in water

love is the sea
where intellect drowns

speak!
o soul of the soul of the soul
o face that renders
every created atom
articulate with love!

➜

I am not Christian, Jew, Pagan, Muslim.
I am not of East nor West; land nor sea.
I am not of nature nor of spirit.
I am not of earth, of water, of air, of fire.
I am not of India, of China, of Bulgaria.
I am not of Iraq nor of Khorasan.
I am not of this world nor of the next world.
I am not of heaven nor of hell.

I am
without body and soul
for He is One only
Beloved

First and Last
Inward and Outward

and I cry,
"One!"
and I cry,
"He is!"

I drained this cup;
there is nothing, now,
but ecstatic annihilation

were I ever other than this
I regret being born

if forever it is this,
I'll trample both worlds!
and dance
ecstatic
forever!

O, Shams,
I am so drunk!
what can I say,

*but I am so drunk
on love*